SAYINGS and PHRASES

ACK! There's a Bug in My Ear!

(And Other Sayings That Just Aren't True)

written by Cynthia Klingel ★ illustrated by Mernie Gallagher-Cole

ABOUT THE AUTHOR

As a high school English teacher and as an elementary teacher, Cynthia Klingel has shared her love of language with students. She has always been fascinated with idioms and figures of speech. Today Cynthia is a school district administrator in Minnesota. She has two daughters who also share her love of language through reading, writing, and talking!

ABOUT THE ILLUSTRATOR

Mernie Gallagher-Cole lives in Pennsylvania with her husband and two children. She uses sayings and phrases like the ones in this book every day. She has illustrated many children's books, including *Messy Molly* and *Día De Los Muertos* for The Child's World®.

The Child's World®

Published in the United States of America
by The Child's World®
1980 Lookout Drive • Mankato, MN 56003-1705
800-599-READ • www.childsworld.com

ACKNOWLEDGMENTS
The Child's World®: Mary Berendes,
Publishing Director

The Creative Spark: Editing

The Design Lab: Kathleen Petelinsek,
Design and Page Production

**LIBRARY OF CONGRESS
CATALOGING-IN-PUBLICATION DATA**
 Klingel, Cynthia Fitterer.
 Ack—there's a bug in my ear! : (and other sayings that just aren't true) / by Cynthia Klingel.
     p. cm. — (Sayings and phrases)
   ISBN-13: 978-1-59296-902-9 (lib. bdg.: alk. paper)
   ISBN-10: 1-59296-902-X (lib. bdg.: alk. paper)
 1. English language—Idioms—Juvenile literature.
 2. Figures of speech—Juvenile literature. I. Title.
 II. Series.
 PE1460.K683 2007
   428.1—dc22   2007004213

People use idioms
(ID-ee-umz) every day.
These are sayings and
phrases with meanings that
are different from the actual
words. Some idioms seem silly.
Many of them don't make
much sense . . . at first.

This book will help you
understand some of the most
common idioms. It will tell
you how you might hear a
saying or phrase. It will tell
you what the saying really
means. All of these sayings
and short phrases—even the
silly ones—are an important
part of our language!

TABLE of CONTENTS

Ants in your pants

It was Friday. Alberto was excited for the weekend. It was his birthday, and he was having a big party. That was all he could think about. Alberto couldn't sit still. He kept getting up and walking around. He had so much energy!

"Alberto!" exclaimed Mr. Baker, his teacher. "What's the matter today? You've got ants in your pants!"

MEANING: To have a lot of energy; to have trouble staying still

At the end of my rope

It had been a long day for Uncle Jim. His car ran out of gas. The dog ran away. The lawn mower wouldn't start. Finally he headed for the house. "I'm at the end of my rope today!" he said to himself.

MEANING: You just can't take any more! You have no more energy to deal with things that are happening.

Bee in your bonnet

"Amanda, if I hear you beg for a puppy one more time, I'll lose my temper!" Dad said with a scowl. "The answer is no. Don't bug me about it anymore!"

"What's the matter?" asked Mom as she walked into the room.

"Amanda's got a bee in her bonnet about getting a puppy," answered Dad.

MEANING: To have an idea that you just can't forget about

5

Blow off steam

Jake was mad. Everything today had gone wrong. He forgot his homework. He spilled his lunch down his shirt. He struck out in softball. He missed the bus going home. Jake was getting angrier and angrier!

"What's the matter?" asked Dad at dinner. Jake couldn't stand one more thing. He told Dad everything that had gone wrong. By the time he was done, Jake was angry again.

"You need to calm down," said Dad. "Why don't you go outside and blow off some steam. You'll feel better. Come back in when you're calm."

MEANING: To have an outburst of angry energy; to get rid of anger

Bug in your ear

Marty and Dad were talking about summer vacation. "This year let's take a trip to the ocean!" said Marty.

"That would be fun," agreed Dad. "I'd love to visit the beach."

"How about Mom?" asked Marty. "Do you think she would like an ocean vacation too?"

"Tell you what," replied Dad. "I'll put a bug in her ear. We'll see if we can get her to start thinking about it."

MEANING: To give someone an idea or to put an idea in someone's head

Cat got your tongue?

Trisha was trying to get Mark's attention. He was ignoring her, no matter what she said. "Come on, Mark. Answer me!" demanded Trisha. "How can I help you if you won't talk?"

Mark looked right at her but didn't say a word.

"What's the matter?" asked Trisha. "Cat got your tongue?"

MEANING: This is a saying we use when a person is not talking or saying anything, especially if they have been asked a question.

A chip off the old block

Grandma watched Gary play with his new puppy.

"I remember you playing like that when you were a boy," said Grandma to Gary's father. "He acts just like you!"

"Yes," replied Gary's father. "Gary's a chip off the old block."

MEANING: To be just like your parent

Cold shoulder

"Can you believe Melissa is having a sleepover and didn't invite us?" asked Rachel.

"I know!" exclaimed Marsha. "We've been her best friends since we were three. Rachel is close friends with Benita now. Ever since Benita moved here, Rachel's been giving us the cold shoulder."

MEANING: To ignore someone in a mean or hurtful way

Cut to the chase

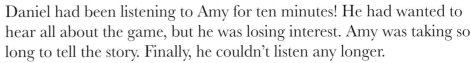

Daniel had been listening to Amy for ten minutes! He had wanted to hear all about the game, but he was losing interest. Amy was taking so long to tell the story. Finally, he couldn't listen any longer.

"Amy," moaned Daniel. "This is the longest story I've ever heard! Just cut to the chase. Did we win or lose?"

MEANING: To get to the point, just say what you mean

The early bird catches the worm

Gus wanted to go to the football game. The problem was that there weren't enough tickets for everyone. They were going on sale tomorrow at 10:00.

The next morning, Gus was dressed and ready to leave the house by 8:00.

"Where are you going?" asked his little brother, Billy.

"I'm going to get in line for football tickets," answered Gus.

"Why so early? You can't get them for two hours!" Billy said.

"That's right," agreed Gus. "But remember, the early bird gets the worm!"

MEANING: If you do something early or ahead of time, you will succeed.

Feather your own nest

Kylie was excited because Mom and Dad were getting new furniture. She couldn't wait to move their old furniture into her room! She ran downstairs to ask Dad when it could all happen.

"What do you mean?" asked Dad. "You and your sister need to share that furniture. You can't have it all. It seems that you are feathering your own nest and not thinking about your sister!"

MEANING: To only think of yourself; to get items, opportunities, or money for yourself without thinking of others' needs

A fly in the ointment

Everything was ready for the party. The balloons were tied with pretty string. The music was playing. The cake was on the counter with the candles ready to be lit. Sophie was so excited! Now the guests could arrive. Suddenly there was a crash in the kitchen. Sophie ran to see what had happened. There was her dog, licking cake and frosting from the floor. He had knocked over the cake! What would Sophie do now?

"Can you believe it?" exclaimed Mom. "I knew there would be a fly in the ointment today!"

MEANING: Something that goes wrong when everything else is in place or is good

Get up on the wrong side of the bed

Justin was eating breakfast when his sister, Jenna, came downstairs. Jenna stomped into the kitchen. She yelled at the dog, made a face at Justin, and slammed the refrigerator door after grabbing some juice.

"What's the matter, Jenna?" asked Justin.

"Just leave me alone!" Jenna said with a scowl.

"Wow! Did you get up on the wrong side of the bed this morning!" exclaimed Justin.

MEANING: To be in a bad mood or to be crabby

Green with envy

"This is so cool!" exclaimed Paul. "I've been wanting this new bike for months!"

"I'm glad you like it," said Mom. "I know you've worked hard to save your money. Are you going to let your brother try it out when we get home? You know he'll be green with envy!"

MEANING: To be very jealous; to want something that someone else has

13

His nose is out of joint

Bryan was ignoring Marcus. Marcus had been elected captain of the team, and Bryan was jealous. Bryan had been sure he would be elected.

"Hey, Marcus!" exclaimed his friend Steven. "There's Bryan. Why won't he walk home with us anymore?"

"Just forget about him for now," sighed Marcus. "His nose is out of joint. I'm hoping he'll be over it by next week. Let's go."

MEANING: To act differently because you are mad or jealous

Keep your chin up

Nina was heartbroken. Her dog had been gone since morning. She was very worried.

"Come on, Nina," said Dad. "Keep your chin up. We'll go looking for Sniffles. He knows the neighborhood. I'm sure he's just having fun with some of the kids."

MEANING: To stay happy or positive, even if it's hard

Lead you by the nose

Antonio was mad. David was always telling him what to do. Today it had gotten Antonio in trouble at school. Now he was trying to explain it to his dad.

"Antonio, you have to start standing up for yourself. You need to make your own decisions," Dad said to Antonio. "Stop letting David lead you by the nose."

MEANING: Letting someone tell you what to do or not do

Loaded for bear

Martin's next door neighbor had not been happy with Martin and his friends for a long time. They were always doing something to annoy him. Today one of the boys had hit a golf ball into Mr. Seegram's window. Mr. Seegram called Martin's dad.

"Was Mr. Seegram really mad?" Martin asked his father.

"Well, he was certainly loaded for bear when he called. I think he settled down a little by the time we finished talking," answered his dad. "But we need to talk about how we can be more respectful of Mr. Seegram and his family."

MEANING: To be very angry or to be ready to take on a tough fight or argument

Many happy returns

Gina was having a great birthday. Her grandparents, aunts, uncles, and cousins were at her house. Everyone played games, laughed together, and enjoyed being with one another. Soon it was time for everyone to go home.

"Happy birthday, Gina! Many happy returns!" Grandma said as she gave Gina a big hug.

"Thank you, Grandma," replied Gina. "This was the best day! It was so much fun."

MEANING: That you will have more happy days just like this one

Mum's the word!

Mum.
Mum.
Mum.

Aaron heard the back door open and close.

"Dad?" asked Aaron. "Is that you?" No one answered. Then Aaron saw Dad tiptoe around the corner. He was holding a huge bouquet of flowers.

"Whoa!" exclaimed Aaron. "Who gets those?"

"Shhh! They're for Mom," whispered Dad. "I'm going to hide them downstairs right now. I want to surprise her after dinner. So please don't tell her. Mum's the word!"

MEANING: To keep a secret

On the tip of your tongue

Hannah answered the phone.

"Hello, Hannah," said her mom's friend Brenda. "Would you please ask your mom which lawn care company comes to your house? I want them to come to our house, too."

Hannah asked her mom. "Hmmm. It's on the tip of my tongue," she replied. "Tell Brenda I'll call her back when I think of the company's name."

MEANING: To have trouble remembering information that you know or to be ready to say something but not able to remember it exactly

Zippy Lawn Care

Out of touch

It had been a long weekend. Ann's parents had gone out of town, and her grandma had stayed with Ann and her brother.

"How was your weekend?" asked Dad when he got home.

"Terrible!" answered Ann. "We couldn't do anything. Grandma was afraid we'd break the computer. All we could watch on TV were little kids' shows. We couldn't have any ice cream or sweets for snacks. We were in bed by eight o'clock!" complained Ann. "It was miserable. Grandma is so out of touch!"

MEANING: To have a gap in information or understanding; not to be clear on what's going on

Pass with flying colors

Sophie had been struggling in English class. To do better, she got extra help from Mr. Voss after class. This morning there had been a big test. Sophie was very worried about how she had done. After school, she went to Mr. Voss.

"Mr. Voss," Sophie said quietly. "Have you corrected my test yet? Could you please tell me how I did?"

"Yes," replied Mr. Voss. "I've corrected your test, Sophie. Congratulations! You passed with flying colors!"

MEANING: To do something very well, or to do it much better than you had to

The pot calling the kettle black

Marnie always had to be first. She always wanted the best things. She had to pick first. She had to be first in line. She wanted the biggest cookie or the best piece of cake. One morning, her brother Brett beat her to the kitchen. Mom had just gotten doughnuts from the bakery. Brett took the biggest doughnut with the most frosting.

"Mom," called Marnie. "Tell Brett to put that doughnut back. He took the best one. He's being selfish."

"Well," said mom, "isn't that the pot calling the kettle black?"

MEANING: When a person acts one way and complains about another person acting the same way

Push the envelope

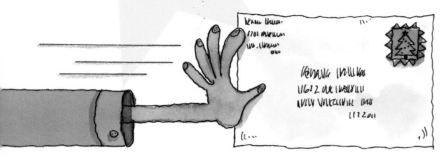

Leo was helping Uncle Matt hang Christmas lights. They were almost done, and there was only a short string of lights left to hang. Uncle Matt looked at it. Could he reach the end without moving the ladder? He stretched and stretched to clip the last two lights to the edge of the roof.

"Careful, Uncle Matt," called Leo. "That doesn't look like a good idea. I think you're pushing the envelope by trying to finish without moving the ladder."

MEANING: To go to the limit. To go as far as it is safe

Rings a bell

"Hello, everyone!" called Dad. He had just gotten home from a business trip. "I met someone you knew a long time ago," he said to Mom. "But she didn't know if you would remember her." He told Mom a story about a woman he'd met in a meeting.

"Hmmm," Mom responded. "I'm not remembering her, but her name does seem to ring a bell."

MEANING: To sound familiar as if you know something about it, but don't remember details

Sitting in the catbird seat

Tryouts for the traveling basketball team were today. Allison had been practicing for weeks. Her jump shot was great. She rarely missed a free throw. She was even hitting three-point baskets!

"Good luck, Allison," Dad said as she got out of the car. "You've worked hard for this. I'd say you're in the catbird seat!"

MEANING: To be in good shape or to be in control

Start the ball rolling

Meredith had a big day ahead of her. It was her job to plant all the vegetable plants and seeds in the garden. Her brother said he'd help her. Meredith wasn't doing a good job of getting started, however. She was wasting time playing with her cat.

"Come on, Meredith. Let's get the ball rolling," suggested her brother. "I want to get this done so we can go to the pool."

MEANING: To get something started

21

Take it with a grain of salt

Sonia was upset. She'd worked very hard on her solo for the school concert. Today she had to miss practice. After school, Sonia's classmate Eva told her that the solo wasn't being included in the program.

"Well, Sonia," sighed her mom after hearing what had happened. "Eva has told you many things in the past that haven't ended up being true. If I were you, I think I'd take Eva's news with a grain of salt and talk to your choir teacher tomorrow."

MEANING: To question something you've been told or not to completely believe something you hear

Tip of the iceberg

Mom knew that Laura and her best friend, Kristin, weren't getting along. It had been going on for weeks. All Mom knew was that Kristin was upset.

"Laura, why don't you tell me why Kristin is so angry with you," suggested Mom. "Maybe I can help."

After Laura explained, Mom left the room, thinking that Kristin had no reason to be so angry with Laura. What Mom didn't know was that Laura's explanation was just the tip of the iceberg.

MEANING: To hear, see, or know only part of something that is much bigger

Under the weather

Stella was hungry. It was Saturday, and every Saturday her mother made waffles for breakfast. But today Mom was late. Stella went upstairs to see what the matter was. She opened her mother's bedroom door and saw that she was still in bed.

"I'm sorry, honey," replied her mom. "I'm feeling a little under the weather this morning. I think I need to get some extra sleep today."

MEANING: To feel sick

Up my alley

Kelsey needed a science fair project. She didn't know what to do. "Mom," said Kelsey. "I need help. I don't know what to do for the science fair."

"Well, you're in luck!" answered Mom. "I used to do science fair projects all the time. I was pretty good at them, too. This is right up my alley!"

MEANING: That something is perfect for you or that you have the skills or interest necessary to do something well

Where there's smoke there's fire

Toby was helping Grandma bake brownies for her party. After the brownies cooled, Grandma and Toby cut them into squares. They packed them into a big box for the party. A little later, Grandma went to put a few more brownies in the box. She saw that half of the brownies were gone!

"Toby!" called Grandma. "Do you know what happened to the brownies?"

Toby came around the corner. There was chocolate smudged around his lips. He had crumbs on his shirt, too. Grandma knew exactly what had happened to the missing brownies.

"Oh, Toby. Where there's smoke, there's fire. I think you do know where they went!" exclaimed Grandma.

MEANING: There are clues that something has happened or that there is a problem